Stage 2

Floppy's Phonics

Liz Miles

Group/Guided Reading Notes

Contents

Introduction 2
Focus phonics 3
High frequency and context words 4
Comprehension strategies 5
Curriculum coverage chart 6

Bug Quiz
Group or guided reading 9
Group and independent reading activities 10
Speaking, listening and drama activities 11
Writing activities 12

Fish and Ships
Group or guided reading 13
Group and independent reading activities 14
Speaking, listening and drama activities 16
Writing activities 16

Now and Then
Group or guided reading 17
Group and independent reading activities 18
Speaking, listening and drama activities 19
Writing activities 20

Eggs
Group or guided reading 21
Group and independent reading activities 22
Speaking, listening and drama activities 23
Writing activities 23

At the Animal Park
Group or guided reading 25
Group and independent reading activities 26
Speaking, listening and drama activities 27
Writing activities 28

Make a Ring Box
Group or guided reading 29
Group and independent reading activities 30
Speaking, listening and drama activities 31
Writing activities 32

Introduction

Welcome to *Floppy's Phonics* Non-Fiction! This series gives you stunning new photographic non-fiction readers linked to *Letters and Sounds*. Your favourite *Oxford Reading Tree* characters guide children through a range of exciting topics, highlighting key features and asking questions to encourage interaction with the text. Children reinforce and practise their decoding skills whilst encountering a range of non-fiction text types and opportunities to make cross-curricular links.

Phonic development

The *Floppy's Phonics* Non-Fiction readers support a synthetic phonics approach to early reading skills. The Stage 2 non-fiction readers are specifically designed for children who are working within Phase 3 of *Letters and Sounds*. They develop children's confidence in segmenting and blending phonemes, and revisit all of the Phase 3 sounds introduced in the *Floppy's Phonics* stories at Stage 2.

The children will benefit most from *Floppy's Phonics* Non-Fiction Stage 2 if they are beginning to:

- recognise most of the Phase 3 letters and sounds, particularly the adjacent consonant sounds
- blend and segment VC, CVC and some CVCC and CCVC words
- develop a bank of high frequency words.

The Stage 2 non-fiction readers can be read in any order for further practise and consolidation of the Phase 3 adjacent consonant sounds. You may wish to read the Stage 2 *Floppy's Phonics* stories with the children to ensure that they have met all the Phase 3 adjacent consonant letters and sounds, before they tackle the non-fiction readers.

The non-fiction readers can also be used alongside core *Oxford Reading Tree* and *Songbirds Phonics* titles at Stage 1+, or for practice and consolidation after introducing the Phase 2 sounds with other programmes.

Focus phonics

Title	ORT Stage Book Band colour Year group	*Letters and Sounds* phase	Phonemes revisited
Bug Quiz	**Stage 2** Red Foundation Stage	3	w x y z zz qu ch sh th ng
Fish and Ships			v w x z qu ch sh th ng
Now and Then			j v w x y ch sh th ng
Eggs			y z qu ch sh th ng
At the Animal Park			j v w y z ch sh th ng
Make a Ring Box			w x y qu ch sh th ng

Most of the words introduced in *Floppy's Phonics* Non-Fiction books at Stage 2 are phonically decodable VC (e.g. *on, up*) or CVC words (e.g. *bug, box*). There are a few CVCC and CCVC words (e.g. *fish, ship*). The other words fall into the following categories in *Letters and Sounds* Phase 3 (see table on page 4):

High frequency tricky words

The few high frequency words that contain unusual or untaught grapheme-phoneme correspondences are termed 'tricky'. Children also need to become familiar with these are soon as possible through regular practice.

Context words

Context words are words which may be phonically regular but make use of phonic patterns not yet introduced (e.g. *penguin*), or are essential for providing meaningful non-fiction information (e.g. *insect*). For *Floppy's Phonics* Non-Fiction Stage 2, these also include the words with long vowel sounds that are encountered in *Letters and Sounds* Phase 3 but are not introduced in the *Floppy's Phonics* stories until Stage 3.

High frequency and context words

Bug Quiz	HF tricky words	we you too for or see look
	Context words	insect food feelers
Fish and Ships	HF tricky words	we you they are see look now for down too
	Context words	sea food
Now and Then	HF tricky words	he she was now you my see look too
	Context words	toy book farm car best
Eggs	HF tricky words	has you they all are her see now look
	Context words	penguin squid born
At the Animal Park	HF tricky words	he we was my look see
	Context words	park chimps
Make a Ring Box	HF tricky words	she you all my for now look too
	Context words	make card foil

Comprehension strategies

Reading is about making meaning, and it is particularly important that a child's reading books offer opportunities for making sense of text. In spite of a limited vocabulary, all the *Floppy's Phonics* Non-Fiction books at Stage 2 are examples of particular genres, e.g. instruction, recount, information. They all have features of non-fiction books, such as a contents page, an index or glossary and illustrations that support the text.

Book title	Comprehension strategy taught through these Group/Guided Reading Notes				
	Prediction	Questioning	Clarifying	Summarising	Imagining
Bug Quiz	✓	✓	✓	✓	✓
Fish and Ships	✓	✓	✓		✓
Now and Then	✓	✓	✓	✓	
Eggs	✓	✓	✓	✓	
At the Animal Park		✓	✓	✓	
Make a Ring Box	✓	✓	✓	✓	

Curriculum coverage chart

	Speaking, listening, drama	Reading	Writing
Eggs			
PNS Literacy Framework (YF)	1.2	W 5.1, 5.6, 5.8 C 7.2	11.1
National Curriculum	Working towards level 1		
Scotland: Curriculum for Excellence (P1)	Early level: LIT 0-01a/LIT 0-11a/ LIT 0-20a LIT 0-02a/ENG 0-03a LIT 007a/LIT 0-16a/ENG 0-17a LIT 0-04a	Early level: LIT 0-12a/LIT 0-13a/LIT 0-21a LIT 0-14a LIT 007a/LIT 0-16a/ENG 0-17a	Early level: LIT 0-01a/ LIT 0-11a/LIT 0-20a ENG 0-12a/LIT 0-13a/ LIT 0-21a LIT 0-26A LIT 0-9b/LIT 0-31a
N. Ireland (P1/Y1)	Listening and responding: 1:1, 3, 4, 5, 9	Engaging with texts: 2: 1, 2, 3, 5, 6, 7	Modelled, shared and guided writing: 3: 1, 2, 3
Wales (Key Stage 1)	Range: 1a, b, 2a, 3a, c, 5 Skills: 1, 2, 4	Range: 1, 2, 3, 4a, f, g Skills: 1a, b, c, 2a	Range: 1, 2, 3, 4 Skills: 2, 3, 5, 8b
Bug Quiz			
PNS Literacy Framework (YF)	8.3	W 5.8, 5.1, C 8.3	11.1
National Curriculum	Working towards level 1		
Scotland: Curriculum for Excellence (P1)	Early level: LIT 0-01a/LIT 0-11a/ LIT 0-20a LIT 0-02a/ENG 0-03a LIT 007a/LIT 0-16a/ENG 0-17a LIT 0-04a	Early level: LIT 0-12a/LIT 0-13a/LIT 0-21a ENG 0-12a/LIT 0-13a/LIT 0-21a LIT 0-14a LIT 007a/LIT 0-16a/ENG 0-17a	Early level: LIT 0-01a/ LIT 0-11a/LIT 0-20a ENG 0-12a/LIT 0-13a/ LIT 0-21a/LIT 0-21b LIT 0-26A
N. Ireland (P1/Y1)	Listening and responding 1: 1, 2, 3, 4, 5, 7, 9	Engaging with texts 2: 1, 2, 3, 5, 6, 7	Modelled, shared and guided writing 3: 3
Wales (Key Stage 1)	Range: 1a, b, 2a, 3a, c, 5 Skills: 1, 2, 4	Range: 1, 2, 3, 4a, f, g Skills: 1a, b, c, 2a	Range: 1, 2, 3, 4 Skills: 2, 3, 5, 8b

Curriculum coverage chart

	Speaking, listening, drama	Reading	Writing
Fish and Ships			
PNS Literacy Framework (YF)	4.1	W 5.5, 5.10, 5.1 C 7.3	10.1
National Curriculum	Working towards level 1		
Scotland: Curriculum for Excellence (P1)	Early level: LIT 0-01a/LIT 0-11a/LIT 0-20a LIT 0-02a/ENG 0-03a LIT 0-04a LIT 0-09a	Early level: LIT 0-01a/LIT 0-11a/LIT 0-20a LIT 0-12a/LIT 0-13a/LIT 0-21a LIT 0-14a LIT 0-19a	Early level: LIT 0-01a/LIT 0-11a/LIT 0-20a LIT 0-12a/LIT 0-13a/LIT 0-21a LIT 0-09b/LIT 0-31a
N. Ireland (P1/Y1)	Listening and responding 1: 1, 2, 3, 4, 5, 6, 7, 9	Engaging with texts 2: 1, 2, 3, 5, 6, 7	Modelled shared and guided writing 3: 1, 2, 3
Wales (Key Stage 1)	Range: 1a, b, 2a, 3a, c, 5 Skills: 1, 2, 4	Range: 1, 2, 3, 4a, f, g Skills: 1a, b, c, 2a	Range: 1, 2, 3, 4 Skills: 2, 3, 5, 8b
Now and Then			
PNS Literacy Framework (YF)	3.1	W 5.8, 5.1, 5.9 C 7.3	11.1
National Curriculum	Working towards level 1		
Scotland: Curriculum for Excellence (P1)	Early level: LIT 0-01a/LIT 0-11a/LIT 0-20a LIT 0-02a/ENG 0-03a LIT 0-07a/LIT 0-016a/ENG 0-17a LIT 0-09a	Early level: LIT 0-01a/LIT 0-11a/LIT 0-20a LIT 0-12a/LIT 0-13a/LIT 0-21a LIT 0-14a	Early level: LIT 0-01a/LIT 0-11a/LIT 0-20a LIT 0-12a/LIT 0-13a/LIT 0-21a LIT 0-26A
N. Ireland (P1/Y1)	Listening and responding 1: 1, 3, 4, 5, 6, 9	Engaging with texts 2: 1, 2, 3, 5, 6, 7	Modelled shared and guided writing 3: 1, 2, 3
Wales (Key Stage 1)	Range: 1a, b, 2a, 3a, c, 5 Skills: 1, 2, 4	Range: 1, 2, 3, 4a, f, g Skills: 1a, b, c, 2a	Range: 1, 2, 3, 4 Skills: 2, 3, 5, 8b

Key

C = Language comprehension   Y = Year   P = Primary

W = Word recognition   F = Foundation/reception

In the designations such as 5.2, the first number represents the strand and the second number the individual objective

Curriculum coverage chart

	Speaking, listening, drama	Reading	Writing
At the Animal Park			
PNS Literacy Framework (YF)	1.4	W 5.9, 5.1, 5.10 C 7.3	11.1
National Curriculum	Working towards level 1		
Scotland: Curriculum for Excellence (P1)	Early level: LIT 0-01a/LIT 0-11a/LIT 0-20a LIT 0-04a LIT 0-09a	Early level: LIT 0-01a/LIT 0-11a/LIT 0-20a LIT 0-12a/LIT 0-13a/LIT 0-21a	Early level: LIT 0-01a/LIT 0-11a/LIT 0-20a LIT 0-12a/LIT 0-13a/LIT 0-21a LIT 0-26A
N. Ireland (P1/Y1)	Listening and responding 1: 1, 3, 9	Engaging with texts 2: 1, 2, 3, 5, 6, 7	Modelled shared and guided writing 3: 1, 2, 3
Wales (Key Stage 1)	Range: 1a, b, 2a, 3a, c, 5 Skills: 1, 2, 4	Range: 1, 2, 3, 4a, f, g Skills: 1a, b, c, 2a	Range: 1, 2, 3, 4 Skills: 2, 3, 5, 8b
Make a Ring Box			
PNS Literacy Framework (YF)	1.4	W 5.5, 5.1, 5.9 C 7.3	11.1
National Curriculum	Working towards level 1		
Scotland: Curriculum for Excellence (P1)	Early level: LIT 0-01a/LIT 0-11a/LIT 0-20a LIT 0-07a/LIT 0-016a/ENG 0-17a LIT 0-04a	Early level: LIT 0-01a/LIT 0-11a/LIT 0-20a LIT 0-12a/LIT 0-13a/LIT 0-21a LIT 0-19a	Early level: LIT 0-01a/LIT 0-11a/LIT 0-20a LIT 0-12a/LIT 0-13a/LIT 0-21a LIT 0-26A
N. Ireland (P1/Y1)	Listening and responding 1: 1, 3, 4, 9	Engaging with texts 2: 1, 2, 3, 5, 6, 7	Modelled shared and guided writing 3: 1, 3, 4, 9
Wales (Key Stage 1)	Range: 1a, b, 2a, 3a, c, 5 Skills: 1, 2, 4	Range: 1, 2, 3, 4a, f, g Skills: 1a, b, c, 2a	Range: 1, 2, 3, 4 Skills: 2, 3, 5, 8b

Bug Quiz

C = Language comprehension	*R, AF* = QCA reading assessment focus
W = Word recognition	*W, AF* = QCA writing assessment focus

Focus phonics

Phonemes revisited in this book: w x y z zz qu ch sh th ng

Group or guided reading

Introducing the book

- W *(Clarifying)* Can the children read the title? Remind the children that the two letters *qu* together make the sound /kw/. Read the title together: *B-u-g Qu-i-z*.
- C *(Clarifying, Prediction)* Encourage the children to talk about any quizzes they have taken part in. What do they expect to find in a quiz?
- W Turn to page 1 and encourage the children to say Floppy's sounds aloud. Which of these sounds can they find on the contents page?
- C *(Clarifying)* Talk with the children about bugs and insects. Ensure they understand that an insect is a type of bug.

Strategy check

Remind the children how the two letters *th* make one sound in *this*. If children cannot sound out a word, encourage them to sound out as much of the word as they can before you explain any tricky letters.

Independent reading

- Ask the children to read the book aloud. Praise and encourage them while they read. Prompt as necessary.
- C *(Questioning)* Ask the children: *How do you know if a bug is an insect?* (An insect has six legs.)
- C *(Clarifying)* When children reach page 16, demonstrate how to use the index.

Ask them to test the index out. Can they find the page that has the word *dots* on it? Also ask: *Where are the answers to the quiz?*

Assessment Check that the children:

- *(R, AF1)* use phonic knowledge to sound out and blend the phonemes in words
- *(R, AF1)* remember how to sound out some of the high frequency tricky words on the inside back cover
- *(R, AF2)* use the information in the text and illustrations to answer the quiz questions correctly.

Returning to the text

W Look at the word *quick* on page 9. Ask: *How many sounds are there?* (3) Ask them to point to the letters that make each sound (*qu-i-ck*). Repeat for *food* on page 11 *(f-oo-d)*.

C *(Summarising)* Ask the children to tell you what the quiz was about.

Assessment *(R, AF1)* Talk about any words the children found tricky and discuss their attempts to work out the words.

Group and independent reading activities

Objective Recognise common digraphs (5.8).

W **You will need:** the text from page 9 written on the whiteboard, i.e. 'This bug has wings. It is quick and it can buzz.'

- Explain that they are going to play another quiz called 'Sounds quiz'.
- Point to 'This' and ask: *Does this word have two sounds?* (No, it has 3.) Repeat the same question for each word on the board.
- Ask the children to show you where to add sound buttons and to identify where two letters represent one sound.

Assessment *(R, AF1)* Do the children remember that the two letters *ng* join together to make the sound /ng/?

Objective Explore and experiment with sounds and words (5.1).

W Write *ee* on the whiteboard. Ask the children to find a word that contains the same sound on page 2 (*see*).

W Turn to page 4. Tell the children that the same sound /ee/ is hidden in a different word on this page (*we*). Can the children read the word from memory?

Assessment *(R, AF1)* Can the children quickwrite the word *we*?

Objective Explore and experiment with sounds (5.1).

W Turn to page 5 and ask the children to find the word *insect*.

- Ask them how many syllables the word has. Encourage them to sound out the word and clap the syllables as they say it.
- Turn to page 11 and ask the children to find another word with two syllables (*looking*). Encourage them to sound out the word and clap the syllables as they say it.
- Can they find any more words in the book with two syllables (e.g. on page 1: *Contents, Begin and Index*).

Assessment *(R, AF1)* Do the children identify the syllables correctly?

Speaking, listening and drama activities

Objective Use language to imagine and recreate roles and experiences (8.3).

C *(Clarifying)* Turn to page 3. Ask the children to say which of the creatures is an insect, and why. Can they name the creatures?

- *(Imagining)* Ask volunteers to pick one of the creatures, and move around like it, making any appropriate sounds.
- Can the other children guess what it is? They are allowed to ask for one clue: e.g. *Are you an insect?*

Assessment *(R, AF2)* Do the children use the answers box on page 3 to check which creatures are insects?

Writing activities

Objective Write labels and captions (11.1).

- **You will need:** drawing paper, white card and string for displaying captions.
- Produce a 'Bug Quiz' for display.
- Turn to pages 2–3 and ask the children to draw a bug from the pages.
- Then ask them to write the question 'Is it an insect?' on a piece of card.
- On the other side of the card they must write the correct answer: 'Yes, this is an insect.' Or 'No, this is not an insect.'
- Display the pictures and pin up the cards on string so the cards can be turned to show the correct answer to the question.

Assessment *(W, AF6)* Do the children remember to include a question mark?

Fish and Ships

C = Language comprehension — *R, AF* = QCA reading assessment focus
W = Word recognition — *W, AF* = QCA writing assessment focus

Focus phonics

Phonemes revisited in this book: v w x z qu ch sh th ng

Group or guided reading

Introducing the book

- C *(Prediction)* Look at the front cover and contents page, and flick through the book. Ask: *What do you think this book is about?*
- W Ask the children to find the title on the cover and point to each sound as they read it together.
- W *(Questioning, Clarifying)* Do the children think the title is funny? Ask: *What other word sounds like 'ships' and often goes with 'fish'?* (chips)
- W Turn to page 1 and encourage the children to say Floppy's sounds aloud. Which of these sounds are in the book title?

Strategy check

If children cannot sound out a word, encourage them to sound out as much of the word as they can before you explain any tricky letters.

Independent reading

- Ask the children to read the book aloud. Praise and encourage them while they read. Prompt as necessary.
- C *(Questioning)* After the children have read each page, ask: *What does the picture show?* Encourage them to point to the picture and explain the details.
- C *(Clarifying)* When the children reach page 16, encourage them to use the index. Ask: *How do we find 'parrot fish' in this book?*

Assessment Check that the children:

- *(R, AF1)* use phonic knowledge to sound out and blend the phonemes in words
- *(R, AF1)* remember how to sound out some of the high frequency tricky words on the inside front cover
- *(R, AF3)* understand that the purpose of the book is to give information.

Returning to the text

(W) Return to words the children found tricky. Together, try to identify the sounds and then blend them together.

Assessment *(R, AF1)* Do the children remember any tricky words from memory, such as *we* on page 4?

Group and independent reading activities

Objective Hear and say sounds in words in the order in which they occur (5.5).

(W) Look at page 14 and ask the children to find words where two letters make one sound. They should find: *ship, this, down, the,* but they may not spot *sea*.

- Identify and practise reading any words that the children missed, saying the sounds in order.
- How many other words can they find in the book with words where two letters make one sound? Divide the pages between the children, giving them one or two pages to search each.

Assessment *(R, AF1)* Do the children blend the phonemes in the correct order, and spot where two letters make one sound?

Objective Use phonic knowledge to make phonetically plausible attempts at more complex words (5.10).

You will need: the following words written on the board *zipping, checking*.

- Ask the children to help you read the words on the board, sounding them out and then blending the sounds.
- Ask the children if they can see a smaller word in each word. Ask what they are (*zip, check*).
- Can the children quickwrite *zipping* and *checking*?

Assessment *(W, AF8)* Do the children use correct spellings?

Objective Explore and experiment with words and texts (5.1).

W **You will need**: word cards to make the sentence 'This quick fish has big fins for zipping along.' Plus cards for: *six* and *now*.

- Put the words in sentence order, leaving gaps for *quick*, *big* and *along*.
- Ask the children to suggest the correct words to fill the gaps. Read the sentence together until it makes sense.
- If necessary, try again until the children are happy with the result.

Assessment *(R, AF5)* Are the children able to explain why a sentence does not make sense?

Objective Show an understanding of how information can be found in non-fiction texts (7.3)

C *(Clarifying)* Explain that you want to find a picture of a hog fish. Ask: *How can I find it in the book quickly?*

- If necessary, demonstrate how to find *hog fish* in the index.
- Hold a class competition to see who is first to find and turn to the correct page for some of the items in the index.
- Ask the children to suggest how to add Wilf to the index. Where would his name go on the list?

Assessment *(R, AF2)* Do the children understand that the index is in alphabetical order?

Speaking, listening and drama activities

Objective Use language to imagine experiences (4.1).

C *(Imagining)* Ask the children to go 'diving' in pairs and talk to each other about what they see.

- Visit each pair and encourage them to start by using vocabulary from the book by asking them, for example: *What sort of fish can you see? What is the fish doing? What is on the sea bed?*

Assessment *(R, AF2)* Do the children refer to ideas from the book?

Writing activities

Objective Attempt writing using forms such as lists (10.1)

- **You will need:** the following word cards: *fish* (6 copies), *box, hog, parrot, dog, cat, fox.*
- Ask the children to make the names of the fish in the book using the cards (*box fish, hog fish, parrot fish*).
- Ask them to make up some more fish names using the other cards, e.g. *fox fish*.
- Ask the children to make up some funny fish names of their own. Ask them to write a list. Who has the funniest fish name?

Assessment *(W, AF1, AF2)* Do children write their made-up fish names clearly?

Now and Then

C = Language comprehension *R, AF* = QCA reading assessment focus
W = Word recognition *W, AF* = QCA writing assessment focus

Focus phonics

Phonemes revisited include: j v w x y ch sh th ng

Group or guided reading

Introducing the book

- **W** Can the children read the title? Remind the children that the two letters *ow* together make one sound (*n-ow*), and *th* together make one sound (*th-e-n*).
- **W** Turn to page 1 and encourage the children to say Floppy's sounds aloud. Which of these sounds are found in the contents list?
- **C** *(Prediction)* Ask the children to look at the pictures in the book. Encourage them to predict what the book is about.
- **C** *(Questioning)* Turn to pages 8–9 and ask the children what is different about the two books in the pictures.

Strategy check

Remind the children to sound out words carefully. If children cannot sound out a word, encourage them to sound out as much of the word as they can before you explain any tricky letters.

Independent reading

- Ask the children to read the book aloud. Praise and encourage them while they read. Prompt as necessary.
- **C** *(Questioning)* Ask the children to explain who the toys or books belong to in each picture and how they differ.

C *(Clarifying)* When children reach page 16, ask them to show you how to use the index. Ask how you can find information about puppets from then and now?

Assessment Check that the children:

- *(R, AF1)* use phonic knowledge to sound out and blend the phonemes in words
- *(R, AF1)* remember how to sound out some of the high frequency tricky words on the inside front cover
- *(R, AF3)* can tell you who each item belongs or belonged to.

Returning to the text

W Can the children find the words *this*, *the* and *then*?

C *(Summarising)* Ask the children to tell you what the book is about. Was their prediction correct?

Assessment *(R, AF1)* Talk about any words the children found tricky and discuss their attempts to work out the words.

Group and independent reading activities

Objective Recognise common digraphs (5.8).

W Write the word *too* on the whiteboard.

- Ask the children to place sound buttons to identify which two letters represent one sound.
- Ask the children to help you find other words in the book that have the same letters that represent one sound (*look, book, too*).
- Can the children think of any other words that use *oo* to represent one sound. Is the sound always the same?

Assessment *(R, AF1)* Do the children notice the different /oo/ sounds in, for example, *look* and *too*.

Objective Read some high frequency words (5.9).

W Write the following words on the board: *he, she, was, you, my.*

- Ask the children to point to the word *she*.
- Ask them how they found the right word. What letter-sounds did they recognize? Did they know the word from memory?
- Sound out the word together then continue in the same way with the other words.

Assessment *(R, AF1)* Do the children recognize which letters make each sound in the words?

Objective Show an understanding of how information can be found in non-fiction texts to answer questions (7.3).

C *(Questioning)* Turn to page 5 and ask the children: *Who had a farm set?* Encourage the children to look in the book and find the answer (Dad).

- Continue with more 'Who', 'What', 'Where' and 'When' questions for the children to answer, such as: page 5, *When did Dad have a farm set?* (He had it when he was six.); page 9, *What can Jim's book do?* (It can pop-up.).

Assessment *(R, AF3)* Do the children refer to the book to find the answers?

Speaking, listening and drama activities

Objective Interaction with others, taking turns in conversation (3.1).

C **You will need**: pictures of toys of different ages, such as Victorian dolls and wooden toys, 60s plastic toys, 70s electronic toys and contemporary toys.

- Encourage the children to take turns to point to one toy and say whether they think it is a toy from the past or now, and why.
- Ask the children to say which toys they think are the oldest, and why.
- Encourage the children to put the pictures in time order, from the oldest to the newest. Encourage them to explain their choices.
- The children could create a timeline of toys for a history display.

Assessment Do the children use appropriate words to explain their views?

Writing activities

Objective Write labels and captions (11.1).

- **You will need:** Sticky notes
- Together read the labels on page 4. Explain that the children are going to write labels to go on more of the pictures.
- Turn to page 6 and ask the children to suggest labels. (e.g. Kipper; car; van; lorry.)
- Ask the children to clearly write a label on a sticky note and place it on the picture. Repeat for other pages.

Assessment *(W, AF8)* Do the children use their phonic knowledge to spell the words correctly?

Eggs

C = Language comprehension	*R, AF* = QCA reading assessment focus
W = Word recognition	*W, AF* = QCA writing assessment focus

Phonics Focus

Phonemes revisited in this book: y z qu ch sh th ng

Group or guided reading

Introducing the book

- W Can the children read the title? Remind the children that the two letters *gg* together make one sound.
- C *(Prediction)* Ask: *What sort of eggs do you think this book is about?*
- W Turn to page 1 and encourage the children to say Floppy's sounds aloud.
- W Read the contents page together. Help the children to sound out the tricky letters *ui* in *penguin*.

Strategy check

Can the children read high frequency decodable words, such as *this* and *are* quickly? If children cannot sound out a word, encourage them to sound out as much of the word as they can before you explain any difficult letters.

Independent reading

- Ask the children to read the book aloud. Praise and encourage them while they read. Prompt as necessary.
- C *(Clarifying)* Discuss the meaning of any words that are new to them.

Assessment Check that the children:

- *(R, AF1)* use phonic knowledge to sound out and blend the phonemes in words
- *(R, AF1)* remember how to sound out some of the high frequency tricky words on the inside front cover

- *(R, AF4)* understand the difference between captions and labels.

Returning to the text

W Can the children find the words *that, this* and *they*?

C *(Summarising)* Ask the children to tell you what the book is about. Can they describe the book in a sentence?

Assessment *(R, AF1)* Discuss any words the children found tricky and discuss their attempts to work out the words.

Group and independent reading activities

Objective Recognise common digraphs (5.8).

W Write the word *look* on the whiteboard.

- Ask the children to place sound buttons to identify which two letters represent one sound: *l-oo-k*.
- Ask the children to help you find other words in the book that have two letters that make one sound.

Assessment *(R, AF1)* Do the children sound out words carefully in order to find two-letter sounds?

Objective Read simple words by sounding out and blending (5.6).

W **You will need:** the whiteboard with the words *the, this, that, they, thing* written on it.

- Encourage the children to sound out the words, ask them to point to the letters as they sound the words out.
- Can they think of any other *th* words? (e.g. *them, then, that, thick, thin, with, moth.*)

Assessment *(R, AF1)* Do the children remember the sounds in the high frequency tricky word *they*?

Objective Explore and experiment with sounds and words (5.1).

- **W** **You will need:** whiteboard
- *(Clarifying)* Challenge the children to find the word in the book with the most sounds (7 sounds - *animals*).
- Write the children's suggestions on the board and ask them to mark the sounds with sound buttons, and then count them.
- Afterwards, ask them to find a word with five sounds, or four sounds.

Assessment *(R, AF1)* Do the children remember to count the sounds rather than the letters?

Objective Extend their vocabulary, exploring the meanings of new words (7.2).

- **C** *(Clarifying)* Tell the children that some readers will not understand the meaning of some of the words.
- Challenge the children to explain in their own words what the following are: *chicks* (page 5); *egg sac* (pages 6–7); *fossil egg* (page 14).

Assessment *(R, AF3)* Do the children refer to the book to find information to help them?

Speaking, listening and drama activities

Objective Use talk to clarify ideas (1.2).

- **C** *(Questioning)* Ask the children to hold a quiz about the book. They should take it in turns to ask a "What", "Why", or "Whose" question and the rest of the group should try to answer it.

Assessment *(R, AF3)* Do the children answer the questions accurately?

Writing activities

Objective Write labels and captions (11.1).

- **You will need:** copies of an outline of Anneena and a speech bubble, large enough for the children to write in.
- Together read the speech bubble on page 3. Explain that the children are going to write speech for Anneena to go on more of the pages.

- Turn to page 5 and suggest that Anneena's sentence starts, 'Look at … .' Encourage the children to finish the caption on their blank copy of Anneena and the speech bubble.
- Turn to pages 10–11 and ask the children to suggest what Anneena might say here. Begin their sentence, then encourage them to complete it in a speech bubble.
- Repeat for other pages.

Assessment *(W, AF8)* Do the children use their phonic knowledge to spell correctly?

At the Animal Park

C = Language comprehension	*R, AF* = QCA reading assessment focus
W = Word recognition	*W, AF* = QCA writing assessment focus

Focus phonics

Phonemes revisited in this book: j v w y z ch sh th ng

Group or guided reading

Introducing the book

- **W** Can the children read the title? Help them sound out the words (*A-t th-e A-n-i-m-a-l P-ar-k*).
- **W** Turn to page 1 and encourage the children to say Floppy's sounds aloud. Which of these sounds are in the contents list?
- **C** *(Questioning)* Flick through the pages and look at the pictures of the animals. Can the children name them all?
- **C** *(Clarification)* Look at the list and page numbers in the index, then ask: *Is this an information book or is this a storybook?* Check they understand that information books have indexes, but storybooks do not.

Strategy check

When reading two- and three-syllable words, remind the children to sound out each syllable in turn. If the children cannot sound out a word, encourage them to sound out as much of the word as they can before you explain any difficult letters.

Independent reading

- Ask the children to read the book aloud. Check they read the labels, too. Praise and encourage them while they read and prompt as necessary.

C *(Questioning)* Ask the group what the children in the book notice about some of the animals they see.

Assessment Check that the children:

- *(R, AF1)* use phonic knowledge to sound out and blend the phonemes in words
- *(R, AF1)* remember how to sound out some of the high frequency tricky words on the inside back cover
- *(R, AF3)* look at the illustrations and read the labels to find information.

Returning to the text

W Look at the word *park* on page 2. Ask: *How many sounds are there?* Ask them to point to the letters that make the three sounds (*p-ar-k*).

C *(Summarising)* Turn to the contents page and ask the children what they can remember about each of the animals.

Assessment *(R, AF1)* Talk about any words the children found tricky and discuss their attempts to work out the words.

Group and independent reading activities

Objective Explore and experiment with sounds (5.1).

W Write the word *animal* on the whiteboard. Ask: *How many syllables does it have?* (3 – an/i/mal)

- Ask volunteers to draw lines to segment the word into its three syllables.

Assessment *(R, AF1, W, AF8)* Can the children spell *animal* correctly using segmentation to help them?

Objective Read some high frequency tricky words (5.9).

W **You will need:** magnetic word cards for *was, My, look*; and the following sentences with words missing:

It ________ a big park.

________ job was to ________ at the map.

- Ask the children to sound out the three high frequency tricky words.

- Then ask them to help you find the correct word for each sentence.

Assessment *(R, AF1)* Are the children able to sound out the high frequency tricky words and read the sentences correctly?

Objective Use phonic knowledge to read simple regular words (5.10).

W **You will need:** the following magnetic word cards scattered on the board: *a*, *looking*, *chimp*, *cubs*, *animal*; and the numbers 1 to 6 written in a list.

- Tell the children that you want to find the word with the most sounds and the word with the fewest sounds.
- Ask volunteers to count the sounds with their fingers as they sound-speak *animal*. Put the card alongside its correct number in the list (6).
- Repeat with the rest of the words.

Assessment *(R, AF1)* Do the children count each of the following as one sound *oo*, *mp, ng*?

Objective Use phonic knowledge to read simple regular words (7.3).

C Ask the children questions about the text and pictures using *where, who, why* and *how*. For example, page 6: *What are the big cats called?*

Assessment *(R, AF3)* Do the children refer to the text and illustrations in their answers?

Speaking, listening and drama activities

Objective Speak clearly and audibly and show awareness of the listener (1.4).

C Turn to pages 12–13 and point to the exclamation marks. Talk about how they show that what is written is exciting.

- Ask volunteers read the sentence in an excited voice.
- Repeat with page 15, encouraging the readers to experiment with the way they read the different sentences.

Assessment *(R, AF5)* Do the children read with appropriate expression taking note of the exclamation mark?

Writing activities

Objective Write labels and captions (11.1).

- **You will need:** a large picture of a zebra or similar animal cut out and pasted onto a piece of paper.
- Ask the children to help you to write labels for different parts of the animal.
- Ask them to help you spell the following labels and decide where to place them: *tail, ear, leg, neck*.
- Encourage the children to suggest a caption for the picture.

Assessment *(R, AF1)* Do the children sound out the words correctly?

Make a Ring Box

C = Language comprehension R, AF = QCA reading assessment focus
W = Word recognition W, AF = QCA writing assessment focus

Focus phonics:

Phonemes revisited in this book: w x y qu ch sh th ng

Group or guided reading

Introducing the book

W Point to the title. Help the children to read the word *make*. Explain that the a-e represents the long vowel /ai/ sound.

W Turn to page 1 and encourage the children to say Floppy's sounds aloud. Which of these sounds are in the contents list?

C *(Prediction)* Flick through the pages and ask the children to predict the subject of the book.

Strategy check

If the children cannot sound out a word, encourage them to sound out as much of the word as they can before you explain any difficult letters.

Independent reading

- Ask the children to read the book aloud. Check they read the labels, too. Praise and encourage them while they read and prompt as necessary.

C *(Questioning, Clarifying)* Now and then at the end of a page, encourage the children to summarise the instructions so far.

Assessment Check that the children:

- *(R, AF1)* use phonic knowledge to sound out and blend the phonemes in words
- *(R, AF1)* remember how to sound out some of the high frequency tricky words

on the inside back cover

- *(R, AF3)* look at the pictures and read the labels to help the children understand the instructions.

Returning to the text

W Look at the word *foil* on page 4. Ask: *How many sounds are there?* Ask them to point to the letters that make each sound (*f-oi-l*). Repeat for *check* on page 9 *(ch-e-ck).*

C *(Summarising)* Turn to the contents page and ask the children what they can remember about each stage in how to make the ring box.

Assessment *(R, AF1)* Discuss any words the children found tricky and discuss their attempts to work out the words.

Group and independent reading activities

Objective Hear and say sounds in words in the order in which they occur (5.5).

W Ask the children to find the word *keep* on page 3. Ask how many sounds are in the word (three).

- Repeat with *egg* on page 4.
- In pairs, ask the children to find and write down as many words as they can from the book that have a repeated letter.
- One child in each pair should find a double-letter word, and the other should write it down, they should then swap roles. The finder must sound out the word so that the writer spells it correctly.

Assessment *(R, AF1, W, AF8)* Can the children sound out and spell the words correctly?

Objective Explore and experiment with words (5.1).

W Write the words *ring* and *sing* on the board. Ask the children to find the sounds that are the same in both (*i, ng*).

- Ask the children to look for words in the book with the same *i* and *ng* sounds (things – pages 2 and 3, going – page 10, fixing – page 13).
- Can the children think of any other *-ing* words, and help you to spell them?

Assessment *(R, AF1, W, AF8)* Do the children use correct spelling?

Objective Use phonic knowledge to read simple regular words (7.3).

C *(Clarifying)* Ask the children to name as many features of the book as possible, e.g. cover, title, contents, heading, page number, list, caption, photo, label, index, glossary.

Assessment *(R, AF4)* Do the children identify features such as labels and headings correctly?

Speaking, listening and drama activities

Objective Speak clearly and audibly and show awareness of the listener (1.4).

- Ask the children to think of other kinds of books or leaflets that give instructions.
- Point out how they all tell you how to do something.
- Ask the children to think of instructions for a leaflet for their PE lesson, for example how to hop, skip or jump.
- They must tell another child in the class how to do it, stage by stage. Are their instructions clear enough for the listener to follow and do the PE activity?
- Children's instructions could be recorded and used in PE lessons to test them out.

Assessment *(R, AF7)* Do the children understand that the book is a 'how to' book, like others they may have seen or read?

Writing activities

Objective Write labels (11.1).

- Explain to the children that they are going to create their own design to decorate the ring box in the book.
- Encourage the children to use ICT to design their decoration. Discuss different materials, such as tinsel, sequins and ribbons.
- Ask the children to draw up and colour their design, then print out if using a computer.
- Ask the children to write labels to describe the different materials they would use. Help them with spelling as necessary.

Assessment *(R, AF2, W, AF2)* Do the children's designs fit the shape of the ring box? Do they label their chosen materials?